ORIGINAL CRYBABY® PRESENTS

THE wah wah BOOK

HAL•LEONARD® CORPORATION
7777 W. BLUEMOUND RD. P.O. BOX 13819 MILWAUKEE, WI 53213

T0050941

CONTENTS

FOREWORD

When certain guitarists play a Wah-Wah, I sometimes wonder if they're doing it for themselves or for the audience. I definitely play mine for myself. Even if our fans hated it I'd still use one, because when it comes to my tone I'm totally selfish! Everytime I step on my Wah-Wah it seems to kick-start my playing because its sound gives me instant inspiration. When the pedal is all the way down (closed) it gives me super aggression and when it's all the way up (open) it adds a fluid coolness. Also, sweeping the thing through its complete tonal range is a great way of accenting certain notes and phrases.

Although the Wah pedal is a hot item right now, it hasn't always been that way. In the mid eighties people were always giving me crap like: "Why are you using that dinosaur thing, man? The Crybaby went out with Jimi Hendrix." I gotta tell ya, that's totally the wrong thing to say to me! Hendrix was a musical genius, and his Wah-Wah work was masterful. Although I really dig what Jimi did with the pedal, the guy who really turned my head around was Brian Robertson, of Thin Lizzy. He had a totally unique technique, and he made me realize that there are stylized ways of using the Wah. Instead of using the pedal to accent individual notes, like most people do, Brian would do long, slow sweeps over a succession of notes to create and augment tension. His solo in "Opium Trail" (*Bad Reputation*) is a classic, and pretty much everything he did on Thin Lizzy's *Jailbreak* album is amazing, too.

Whenever I play my Wah I always try to do everything I've ever learned to do with it in one solo! In addition to accenting notes and phrases, I also try to utilize its broad scope of tones. I used my Wah-Wah pedal a lot on the last Metallica studio album (*Metallica*), and sometimes our producer, Bob Rock, would purposely hide the thing so I wouldn't be able to use it that day! Invariably, though, after a while I'd start getting itchy feet and would end up having to search the whole damned studio for my Wah-Wah while Bob laughed at me!

There are a lot of great things you can do with a Crybaby, and anyone who dismisses it as being a one-dimensional effect obviously hasn't looked or listened deeply enough. To me, the Wah-Wah is a tonal crayon you can use to color a great many aspects of your playing, and it's right there at your feet! I love this pedal to death. In fact, the only way you could keep me from playing one is by chopping off my legs!

Kirk Hammett
December 1993

3

INTRODUCTION

Why a Book on Wah?

(**Important note**: The first sentence of this piece has to be read using your best **Clint "Dirty Harry" Eastwood** voice!)

"I know what you're thinking, punk! How on earth can a 48-page book be dedicated to an effect pedal as stupidly simple as a Wah-Wah?" Well, my friend, the best way for me to answer that question is with another question: Apart from being truly great guitarists, what do Jimi Hendrix (R.I.P.), Jimmy Page, Eric Clapton, Jeff Beck, Stevie Ray Vaughan (R.I.P.), Robin Trower, Carlos Santana, Randy Rhoads (R.I.P.), Michael Schenker, Eric Schenkman (Spin Doctors), Diamond Darrell (Pantera), Tommy Bolin (R.I.P.), Edward Van Halen, Slash, Jerry Cantrell (Alice In Chains), Joe Satriani, Eric Johnson, Dan Spitz (Anthrax), Mike McCready (Pearl Jam), Steve Vai, and Kirk Hammett (Metallica) all have in common? The answer is this: They've all been known to utilize a Wah-Wah to enhance their unique playing styles. Furthermore, every time they step on the thing they manage to squeeze an almost infinite palate of highly desirable tonal colors and inflections out of it.

In my humble opinion, folks, the Wah-Wah is a multi-dimensional tonal device that's capable of creating magic far beyond the "whacka-whacka" effect that helped make Isaac Hayes' "Theme From Shaft" so memorable. Now, please don't get me wrong here, I'm not trying to tell you that "whacka-whacka" noises aren't cool—hell, Jimi Hendrix proved that they can be God-like by using them in his "Voodoo Child (Slight Return)" (*Electric Ladyland*) intro way back in 1968! All I'm trying to say is that there's a lot more to this seemingly straightforward pedal than maybe first meets the eye, or should I say ear! And, in a nutshell, that's what this book is all about.

As I'm sure you know, the ultimate goal of many guitarists is being able to emulate the unique inflections of the human voice. And that's one of the biggest attractions of the Wah-Wah pedal—the fact that a skillful player can use the thing to help make the guitar talk. Why else do you think the name Crybaby was born! As our eloquent Foreword author, Kirk Hammett, so aptly puts it: "The Wah-Wah pedal can help make your guitar work sound more 'human' because it makes you play more emotionally and conversationally. I often use my Wah to transform certain notes into gut-wrenching screams and cries. This can be done because the Crybaby enables you to vary the timbre of whatever you're playing, in the same way that you use your mouth to form different vowel sounds." Two jaw-dropping examples of axemen employing a Crybaby to make their strings speak are Jimi Hendrix's opening to "Still Raining, Still Dreaming" (*Electric Ladyland*) and Steve Vai's tongue-in-cheek "conversation" with David Lee Roth during the intro to "Yankee Rose" (*Eat 'Em And Smile*).

In the pages that follow we'll delve into a few of the many different ways this great effect pedal can be used by studying some classic examples of it in action—like the unforgettable opening to Hendrix's "Burning Of The Midnight Lamp" (*Electric Ladyland*), Eric Clapton's haunting Wah-Wah chord work in "White Room" (*Wheels Of Fire*), and Kirk Hammett's mayhemic majesty in Metallica's "Enter Sandman" (*Metallica*). Then, armed with this knowledge, we're ready to learn no fewer than nine Wah-Wah-drenched solos by the following six-string stars: Jimi Hendrix, Eric Clapton, Stevie Ray Vaughan, Zakk Wylde (Ozzy Osbourne), Mike McCready (Pearl Jam), Kirk Hammett, Jerry Cantrell (Alice In Chains), Slash, and Edward Van Halen. Now, is that an impressive list or what!?

If you're a big fan of the Crybaby, then what you've just read will have caused you to drool all over yourself in a manner befitting Pavlov's dog! So, what are you waiting for? Grab your axe, amp, and trusty Wah-Wah and let's get busy!

CHAPTER 1

Wah's Up, Doc?

Where the Wah Came From

The Wah-Wah pedal was invented by in 1967 by two guys named Bradley Plunkett and Lester Kushner. At the time Plunkett, a 25-year-old engineer for Warwick Electronics (a division of Whirlpool, a major corporation that owned both Thomas Organ and Vox), was working on a less expensive replacement for the three-position voicing switch on Vox amps. Kushner threw in a few ideas, and after Brad has messed with the design, the very first primitive Wah-Wah circuit was born. According to legend, when a test was done using a guitar, it sounded so cool that people came running in to see what was going on. The circuitry was then put into a reworked volume pedal and, as the saying goes, the rest is history!

When Vox first launched the unit it was being built in Italy and was called The Clyde McCoy Wah-Wah pedal. For your information, McCoy was a famous trumpet player whose 1931 hit "Sugar Blues" first popularized the "Wah-Wah" sound of the muted trumpet. Vox used his name on their pedal as a marketing effort, to clarify the sound it produced. The name "Crybaby" came into effect when they wanted another brand name to sell through the wholesale distribution channels in the music business. The unit didn't change one iota; just the name did. When the Vox company went under, there was no sales team to sell the Vox pedals. The Crybaby survived because it was still being sold by the wholesalers.

Since its birth the Wah-Wah has become the most stepped-on guitar effects pedal of all time. It is also responsible for helping to spice up some of rock guitar's most memorable moments—a complete listing of which would take up a great many pages! It was also employed by pretty much every disco/funk/soul axeman in the seventies and, despite its appearance on some truly horrendous rubbish, some pretty cool Wah-Wah stuff did come out of the disco boom—like Isaac Hayes' "Theme From Shaft," the Temptations' "Papa Was A Rolling Stone," and Wild Cherry's "Play That Funky Music," to name but three.

Probably as a direct result of overexposure, the popularity of the Wah-Wah declined drastically in the late seventies and early eighties. Having said this, rockers such as Eric Clapton, Stevie Ray Vaughan, Michael Schenker, Robin Trower, and Randy Rhoads stuck with the thing, and as the eighties progressed, a new generation of big-name players started latching on to the pedal, including Slash of Guns N' Roses, Kirk Hammett of Metallica, and Zakk Wylde of Ozzy Osbourne. Then, as the nineties hit, so did a huge retro movement in rock. Consequently, the Wah-Wah is currently enjoying a massive resurgence. Indeed, many of today's cutting-edge players consider the pedal to be an essential part of their gear. Thus, the effect can frequently be heard being used in the tunes of hard-hitting bands such as Pearl Jam, Faith No More, Alice In Chains, White Zombie, Pantera, Prong, Sepultura, and, of course, Metallica and Guns N' Roses. Three of the biggest new names in rock guitar—Joe Satriani, Eric Johnson, and Steve Vai—are also major advocates of the unit.

Although many different companies have dabbled with Wah-Wah production over the years (apparently, by the late sixties there were some 50 manufacturers worldwide!), the **Crybaby** and **Vox** pedals have always set the standard by which all others are judged. In 1982, **Jim Dunlop Manufacturing** procured the Crybaby tooling, patents, and trademarks. Dunlop currently offers eight different versions of this mythical pedal, including a Jimi Hendrix series. The latest development is the Rack Mount version with multiple remote controller pedals. We'll be looking at all these shortly.

How the Wah Works

In a nutshell, a Wah-Wah is kinda like a "souped-up" tone control that sits on the floor. Two of the most important components in the pedal are a *bandpass filter* and a *potentiometer*. So, in order to under-stand a bit more about the inner workings of a Wah-wah, you have to have a grasp on what these two things do.

For all intents and purposes, a bandpass filter can thought of as an amplifier that only boosts the frequencies in its *resonant frequency* range. All frequencies that fall above or below this range are rejected—*i.e.*, not allowed to pass. Hence the name "bandpass filter"—the filter only allows a certain band of frequencies to pass through it and get boosted. Geddit? Good, now let's get on to the next step.

The majority of Wah-Wahs use a bandpass filter that has a variable resonant frequency, which is controlled by a potentiometer (frequently referred to as a *pot*). This potentiometer is linked to the pedal so you can alter the resonant frequency of the bandpass filter with your foot. (Hold your Crybaby at eye level and you'll be able to see exactly how the pot gets rotated as you open and close the pedal.) So, whenever you open or close the pedal slightly, a different range of frequencies gets boosted. When the pedal is pushed all the way down (closed), the high fequencies (treble) get boosted. Conversely, when the pedal is all the way up (opened), the low frequencies (bass) are the ones that are emphasized.

Where Should I Put It?

Where should you place your Wah-Wah relative to your other stomp boxes? Here are a few guidelines that you may find helpful:

a) Most players put their Wah-Wah pedal before any time-based or ambient effects such as reverb, delay/echo, chorus, flange, and vibrato. They do this 'cos they want to add these effects to their Wah-Wah sound and not vice-versa. This makes a lot of sense if you think about it.

b) To the vast majority of axemen, placing a Wah-Wah in the effects loop of an amp is a major "no-no!" The reason for this is simple: It sounds terrible!

c) Distortion followed by Wah sounds very different from Wah followed by distortion. The former (distortion, then Wah) causes the Wah-Wah to make a very overstated, duck-like "quacking." The opposite way around (Wah, then distortion) is much more subtle. As you will find out in the next section, Dunlop makes a couple of combination Fuzz/Wah pedals that have a switch that allows you to decide which effect comes first.

d) Ignore all of the above, experiment with where you put the Wah in your signal path, and let your ears decide what sounds best!

Which Wah's Right for Me?

As already mentioned earlier in this chapter, Dunlop makes a grand total of eight different Wah-Wah pedals. This number is made up of six types of Crybaby (including the Rack Mount system, which we'll omit for right now, since it's in a class by itself!) and two types of Jimi Hendrix Wahs. In addition to all being black, their common features are as follows: Heavy die-cast construction; a weight of 3.7 lbs. (except the GCB-95FW Crybaby Fuzz Wah, which is 3.8 lbs.); dimensions of 10" x 4" x 2.5" (LxWxH); and requiring a 9-volt battery or external power to operate.

Here's a quick breakdown of what each one of these different units is capable of:

A. The Crybaby Pedal Series

The GCB-95 Crybaby Wah Wah Pedal
This is the original Crybaby that's favored by such greats as Jimi Hendrix, Eric Clapton, Steve Vai, and Joe Satriani. It contains a 100k ohm Hot Potz potentiometer that makes that classic quick, abrupt Wah sound possible.

The GCB-95O Crybaby Octave Wah Pedal
This pedal has a modified Wah effect plus an Octave Fuzz that can be smooth and subtle, wild and piercing, or anything in between! You can have three choices of effect: Wah, Octave Distortion, or both together. Two LEDs at the front of the unit let you know exactly what's going on: Green is for Wah and Red is for the octave fuzz. The pedal also has two external control knobs: one is for the volume and the other is for the tone of the distortion. The Octave Distortion on/off switch is located at the right rear side of the pedal; the toe switch is for the Wah.

The GCB-95FW Crybaby Fuzz Wah Pedal
As well as containing Wah, this pedal houses a specially designed analog distortion effect that is foot controllable from a light, bluesy edge to raunchy rock. Just like the GCB-95O, you have two LED indicators (Green for Wah, Red for Fuzz) and three effect choices: Fuzz, Wah, or both together. What's even cooler is this: an external switch allows you to pre-set the fuzz before or after the Wah. This means you have a total of four effect options—think about it!

The GCB-95 Bass Crybaby Pedal
This one's designed specifically to add Wah to the lower frequency range of the bass guitar.

The Crybaby 535 Series Wah Pedal
Dunlop's 535 Series offers the ultimate in vintage Wah tone. This pedal is equipped with a carefully selected inductor for a warm harmonic tone and a low-source-impedance line driver to improve your signal-to-noise ratio.

The CR1S Rack Mount Single Channel Wah-Wah System
The first rack mountable Wah System utilizing the legendary Crybaby Wah effect. Key features include:
- High, Middle, and Low Wah range setting
- Soft effect switching utilizing hi-reliability hardware
- Four controller input compatibility on one channel allowing Wah accessibility at multi-stage locations
- Independent EQ Circuit offering Mid and Low Range adjustments
- Option for wet and dry outputs
- Front panel illuminators indicating back panel analog connections

B. The Hendrix Wah Pedal Series

The JH-1 Jimi Hendrix Wah Wah Pedal
This pedal is exact reissue of the renowned, original sixties Thomas Organ design with modified circuitry that lowers the frequency of the operating range and, in so doing, produces a fatter, more open sound.

The JH-1FW Jimi Hendrix Fuzz Wah Pedal
As well as having Hendrix Wah, this beast boasts a distortion circuit that has been designed to duplicate the fuzz sound Jimi used in the sixties. In terms of features, this one's identical to the GCB-95FW: foot controllable distortion intensity, two LEDs, and four effects choices—Wah, Fuzz, Wah before Fuzz, or Fuzz before Wah.

Whew! If you're looking for a new Wah there's definitely one in there for you. Anyhow, enough of this yapping! Let's go...

CHAPTER 2

Wah This Way!

"Using a Wah-Wah is real easy...right? All you have to do is switch the damned thing on and then move your foot up and down. There's nothing to it!"

The above statement was, believe it or not, made by a friend of mine named Dave when he found out I was writing this book. He wasn't kidding, either; he was dead serious! Well, in fairness to Dave, he's not 100% wrong; he just happened to omit an important fact or three! Here's what I think he actually should have said:

"It's easy to use a Wah-Wah...what's hard is using one well!"

Sure, all you have to do to work a Wah is move your foot up and down, but it's a tad more involved than that. There's a definite art involved. To use the Wah-Wah skillfully you have to decide exactly when it is best to open or close the pedal and also how quickly or slowly you should do so! Hey, sometimes it's best to just let the thing stay half-open for a while!

Yep, like a lot of things in life, using a Wah-Wah well is all down to timing! So, before getting into the solos, let's explore a few of the many ways you can Wah...

Foot-Tapping Fun!

When you first step on a Wah-Wah, the instinctive thing to do is open and close the thing by tapping your foot to the beat of the music. This can sound really cool, but, as you've probably already discovered, it gets old real quick if it's all you do! If you listen carefully to the masters of the Wah in action, it doesn't take long to realize that they also frequently do things with the pedal that are far less obvious from a rhythmic point of view. Check out the opening 12 bars of Jimi Hendrix's "Voodoo Child (Slight Return)" (*Electric Ladyland*) and you'll hear exactly what I'm talking about. By continually altering the pedal's rate of motion, Hendrix uses the Wah-Wah to dramatically enhance the song's intro. We'll be looking at exactly what Jimi does with his foot during this epic burst of Wah-Wah excellence shortly. Before studying this *pièce de résistance*, however, I suggest we look at a few slightly easier examples of the pedal in action.

Before we go any further, I guess I should show you the Wah-Wah notation we'll be using:

+ = pedal fully closed/toe down (treble)

o = pedal fully open/toe up (bass)

o < + = smoothly sweep pedal from fully open to fully closed

+ > o = smoothly sweep pedal from fully closed to fully open

Thus, Figure 1 instructs you to smoothly open and close the pedal by tapping your foot in time so that the pedal is fully closed on each downbeat (*i.e.*, on counts "1," "2," "3," "4") and fully open on each upbeat (*i.e.*, the "and" of each count; "1 and," "2 and," "3 and," "4 and").

Figure 1

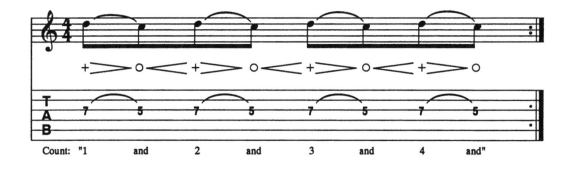

Count: "1   and   2   and   3   and   4   and"

As already mentioned, this simplistic, foot-tapping Wah-Wah motion can be very effective on occasions. If you don't believe me, check out Figure 2, which is the intro from "Up From The Skies" (*Axis: Bold As Love*). Hey, if it's OK by Jimi, then it's OK by me!

Figure 2

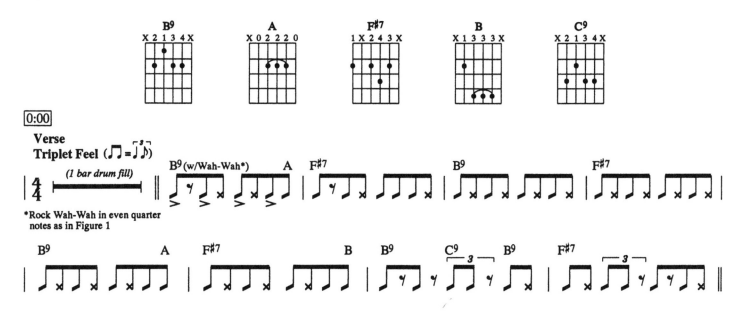

The foot-tapping approach works real well on lead work, too, as Jimi proves in Figure 3, which is taken from his outro solo in the same song, "Up From The Skies." We'll be studying this lead break more a little later on, too. If you home in on Hendrix's Wah-Wah work closely, you'll hear him use this approach quite a bit—like during his killer version of Bob Dylan's "All Along The Watchtower" (*Electric Ladyland*), for instance.

Figure 3

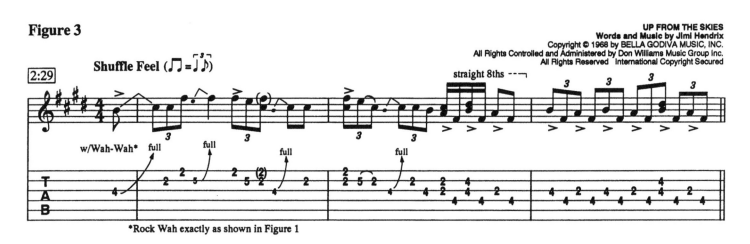

9

Tapping out time with your Wah-Wah like this can be a great way of adding extra excitement to a lightning-fast repeated lick that is moved chromatically (one fret at a time) up the neck. Figure 4 is a good example of what I'm talking about. Carlos Santana often does this type of thing.

Figure 4

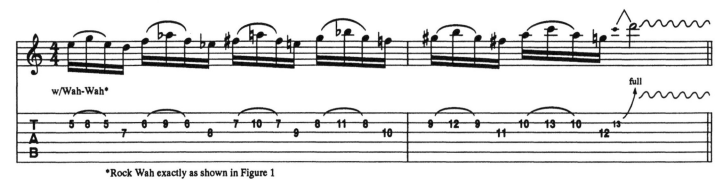

*Rock Wah exactly as shown in Figure 1

Here's one more great example that uses this basic foot-tapping ploy to great effect. Figure 5 is very similar to the repeated Wah-Wah motif that Tommy Victor of Prong uses to open "Broken Peace" (*Cleansing*). Here he combines a funky, distorted D5 chord with some percussive "whacka-whacka" sounds that he creates by muting his strings and then strumming them in the rhythm indicated while opening and closing his Wah exactly as in Figure 1.

Figure 5

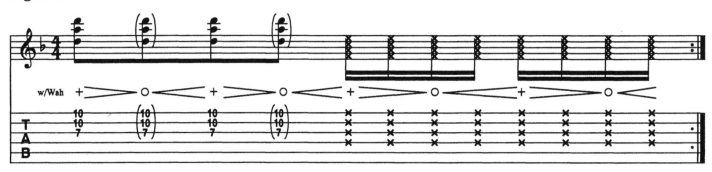

Percussive Pedaling

Using a Wah to create percussive color like this can really add dimension and depth to the rhythmic groove of a track. If you listen carefully to "Broken Peace" you'll hear Figure 5 being repeated throughout much of the song. It's way back in the mix, but its impact is nevertheless dynamic. Many funk bands employ the Wah in this way, including current monster group The Red Hot Chili Peppers. You can create many interesting rhythmic patterns by doing this. In fact, you can treat the pedal almost like it's a hi-hat. Figure 6 is a Wah-Wahed, "whacka-whacka" motif that apes the hi-hat pattern used to kick off Jeff Beck's "Blue Wind" (*Wired*).

Figure 6

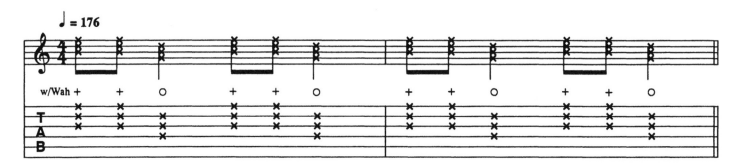

Other well-known instances of percussive "whacka-whacka" in action include the beginnings to Hendrix's "Voodoo Child (Slight Return)" (we'll be looking at this later on) and Robin Trower's "Too Rolling Stoned" (*Bridge Of Sighs*). Guns N' Roses use this technique to begin "Mr. Brownstone" (*Appetite For Destruction*), as shown in Figure 7. Notice how even this fairly simple pattern has a hypnotic effect on the listener.

Figure 7

*strum muted strings in rhythm indicated

Try experimenting with some percussive Wah-Wah work in your own songs, especially in the recording studio when you find yourself with a spare track or two to play with. As Prong's "Broken Peace" proves, sometimes a subtle, well-thought-out "whacka-whacka" rhythm that's placed towards the back of the mix can make a world of difference to the rhythmic feel and groove of a certain section or passage. Having stated this, please be frugal. As is often true, it's possible to have too much of a good thing! Anyway, let's get back to some more foot-tapping type fun...

Reverse It!

Another neat little thing you can do with the Wah while merely tapping out time is reverse the movement of your foot so the pedal is fully open (up) on each downbeat and fully closed (down) on each upbeat, as shown in Figure 8. If it takes you a try or two to get used to this, don't worry; but be warned: "You ain't seen nothing yet!"

Figure 8

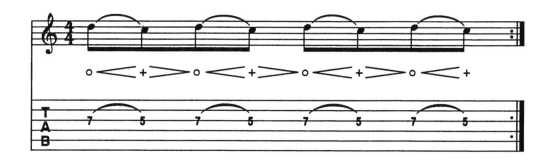

The difference this slight change of the foot-tapping approach has on how your Wah-Wah work sounds is surprisingly noticeable. Listen to how different the same exact lick sounds using both approaches by playing Figures 9a and 9b back to back.

Figure 9a   **Figure 9b**

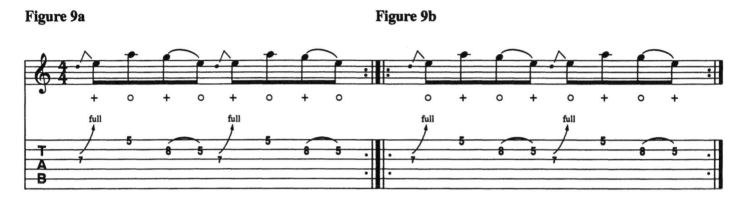

You can hear this "reversed" foot-tapping technique being used by Eric Clapton during the verses of Cream's "Tales Of Brave Ulysses" (*Disraeli Gears*), as shown in Figure 10.

Figure 10: "Tales Of Brave Ulysses," by Eric Clapton and Cream (verse excerpt)

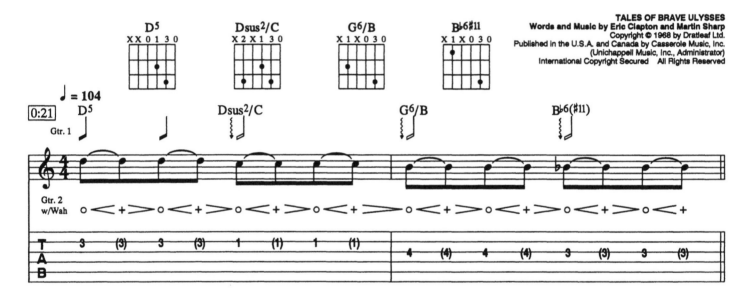

E.C. adopts the same exact pedal movement in two other places in this song—on a sustained A7 chord at the end of verse 1 (Fig. 11) and on the sustained D note at the start of the outro solo (Fig. 12).

Figure 11: "Tales Of Brave Ulysses," by Eric Clapton and Cream (excerpt)

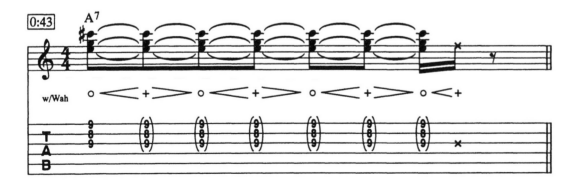

12

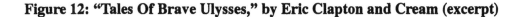

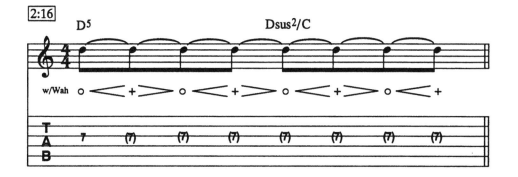

Faster, Pussycat!

By speeding up the rocking action of your Wah-Wah to a rapid flutter, a tremolo-like effect is produced that can sound great when used on sustained chords. The best known example of this is, without any shadow of a doubt, the pre-chorus of "White Room" by Eric Clapton and Cream (Fig. 13).

Figure 13 (Pre-Chorus excerpt)

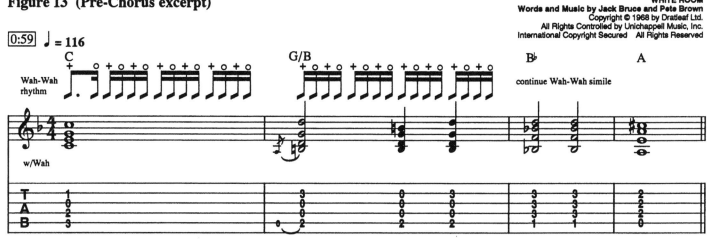

Two further illustrations of this tremolo-like Wah-Wah effect can be found in the intro to "Why Go" (*Ten*) by Pearl Jam and in "Mr. Brownstone" (*Appetite For Destruction*) by Guns N' Roses (Fig. 14).

Figure 14: "Mr. Brownstone" (excerpt)

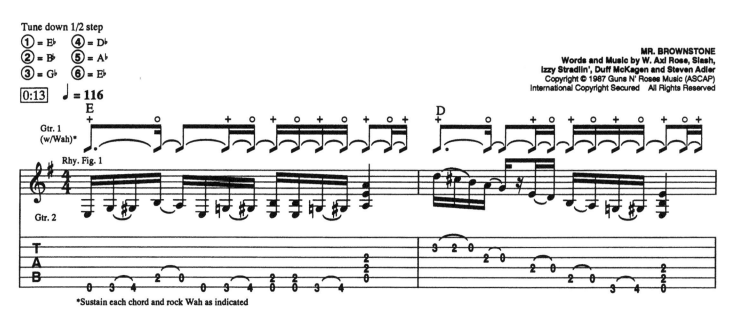

*Sustain each chord and rock Wah as indicated

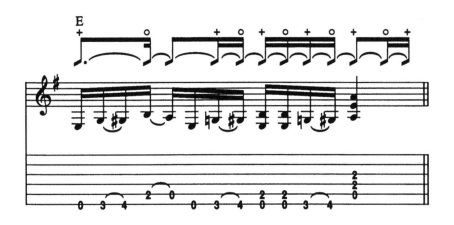

Causing your Wah to flutter like this can also be very effective on lead work every now and then. Jimi Hendrix's cosmic solo in "Burning The Midnight Lamp" (*Electric Ladyland*) is packed full of rapid Wah-Wah movement, and Mike McCready of Pearl Jam can be heard employing it in Figure 15, a happening little fill from "Even Flow" (*Ten*).

Figure 15: (Lead Guitar Fill)

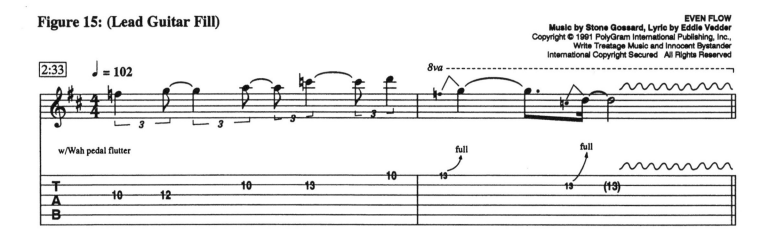

Slow Down, Dude!

As Kirk Hammett pointed out in his highly entertaining foreword, sometimes just slowly sweeping your Wah open or closed can be extremely effective. Check out how the lick you played in Figures 9a and 9b sounds when you slow down your Wah-Wah sweep rate to the one shown in Figure 16.

Figure 16

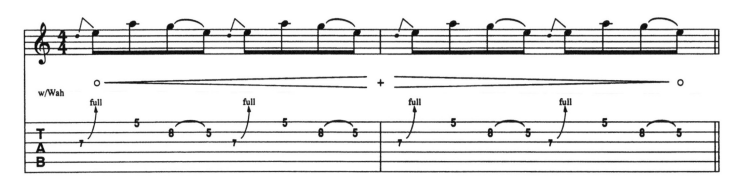

Jerry Cantrell takes full advantage of slow, deliberate Wah-Wah sweeps during the first half of his "Man In The Box" (*Facelift*) solo. For the first two bars he slowly opens and closes his Crybaby while performing a two-note trill on the A string (Fig. 17). Then in the fifth bar he slowly closes the pedal while repeatedly picking a single bent note (Fig. 18). As you will hear, the tension created by these slow but sure Wah-Wah maneuvers is very effective indeed.

Figure 17

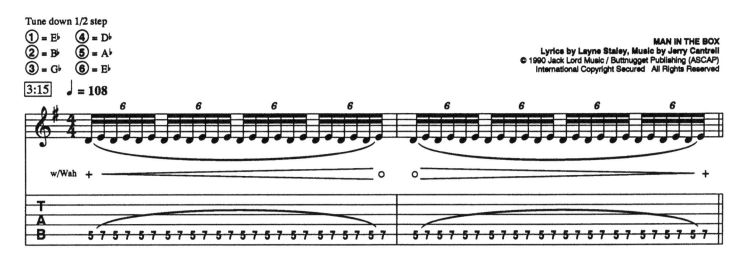

Figure 18: "Man In The Box" (solo excerpt)

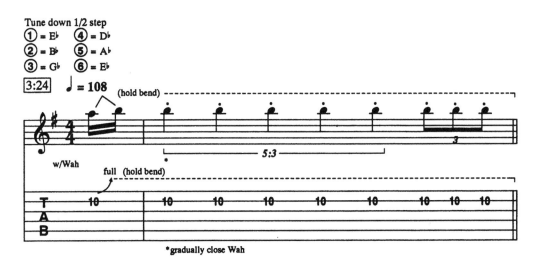

*gradually close Wah

Figure 19 is taken from the end of the live version of Ozzy Osbourne's head-banging favorite, "I Don't Know" (*Ozzy Osbourne, Randy Rhoads Tribute*). Here the late, great Randy Rhoads switches on his Wah and then slowly opens it while sustaining an open G5 power chord. By doing this he adds a whole new dimension to the part.

Figure 19

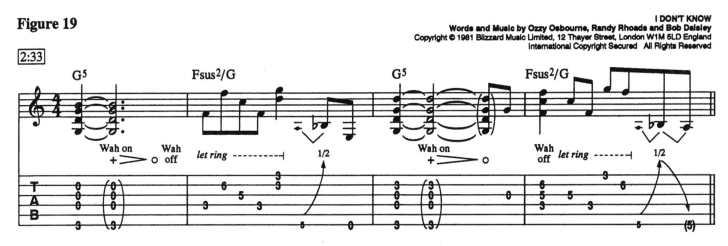

When Less Is More!

As Figure 19 illustrates well, you don't have to have your Wah "on" for a very long time in order for it to weave its magic. Less can sometimes mean more and, on occasions, brief bursts of Crybaby can be much more dramatic than using the pedal for an extended period. Figure 20 shows how Stevie Ray Vaughan quickly switches his Wah-Wah on and off during his electrifying version of "Voodoo Child (Slight Return)" (*Couldn't Stand The Weather*). By doing this he adds searing bite to a certain notes, causing them to virtually leap out of the track and grab you by the throat! You can also hear the tune's composer, Jimi Hendrix, doing this to great effect to bring the original studio version of this song to a climactic close.

Figure 20: "Voodoo Child (Slight Return)" (excerpt from Stevie Ray Vaughan's studio version)

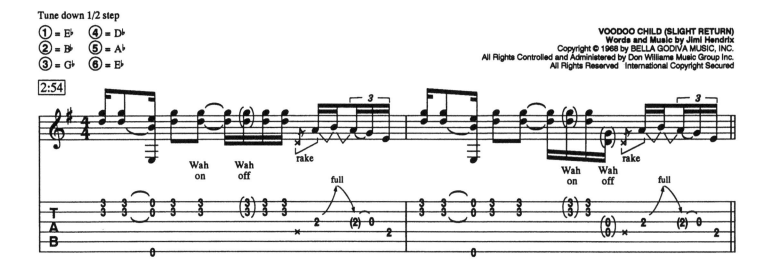

Hold It Right There, Buster!

For certain runs and licks you don't have to move your Wah-Wah at all in order for it to sound great. Instead you find a position in the pedal's range that enhances your tone in a desirable way and then leave it there. By doing this you're using your Wah as a tone filter. The gentleman most noted for this type of Crybaby employment is that Teutonic six-string legend, Michael Schenker. Many of his highly praised lead tones were attained by him leaving his Wah-Wah half-open at a tonal "sweet spot."

In addition to Michael, other players that adopt this tone filter approach from time to time include Randy Rhoads and Joe Satriani. If you listen to Joe closely you'll realize that he does this a lot. The following quote from the man explains exactly why: "For me, the Crybaby is an extension of the electric guitar. It's the ingredient for a great tone."

Figure 21 is bars 5 to 8 of Randy's intro to the studio version of "I Don't Know" (*Blizzard Of Oz*). Figure 22 is a short burst of lead taken from Joe's spine-tingling instrumental "Circles" (*Surfing With The Alien*). The sweet spots that six-string stars like Schenker, Satriani, and Rhoads use to their tonal advantage all lurk within the sweep range of your Wah pedal, and they're easy to find, too. All you have to do is use those wonderful audio devices we were all born with—your ears!

Figure 21

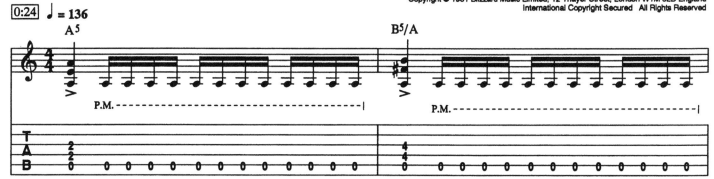

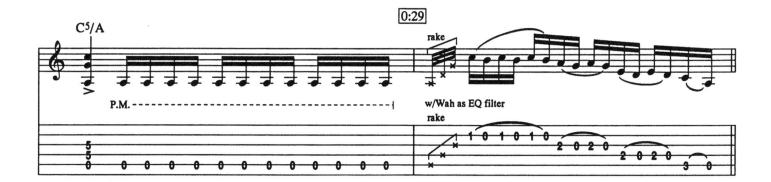

Figure 22

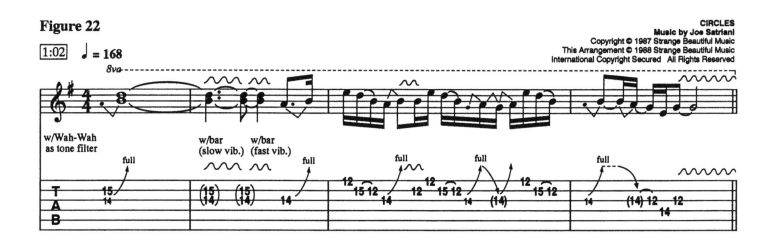

Incidentally if you're a big Clapton fan, it might interest you to know the following: In the March 1993 issue of *Guitar Player* magazine, Cesar Diaz, a guy who was Eric's amp technician and gear adviser, revealed that some of E.C.'s most talked about sounds were often created by using a Wah-Wah as a tone filter. I quote: "...a lot of Clapton's 'woman tone' was created this way, with the pedal rocked about three-quarters back from the full forward position."

One Wah Per Note!

Before touching on a couple of slightly more complex Wah-Wahing ways, I should quickly touch on a pretty common technique: one pedal depression per note. This is a great way of using the Wah, and consequently many great players can be heard doing it on a regular basis. For example, Hendrix can be heard employing this technique during much of his "Burning of the Midnight Lamp" intro (Fig. 23).

Figure 23

This one-depression-per-note Wah-Wah tactic is often used in conjunction with unison string bending, a technique that involves playing an unbent note on one string while bending a note on the next lowest string up to the same exact pitch. Both notes are picked simultaneously. A guy who combines unison bends and the Wah-Wah a lot is White Zombie's talented axe-wielding maniac, J. Yuenger. Figure 24 is similar to a Wah-Wahed oblique bend ascent J. hits us with during his second solo in "Black Sunshine" (*La Sexorcisto: Devil Music Vol. 1*). This dramatic, cutting climb is made even wilder thanks to some pretty outrageous whammy bar abuse.

Figure 24

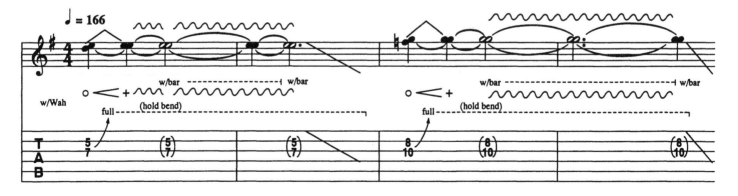

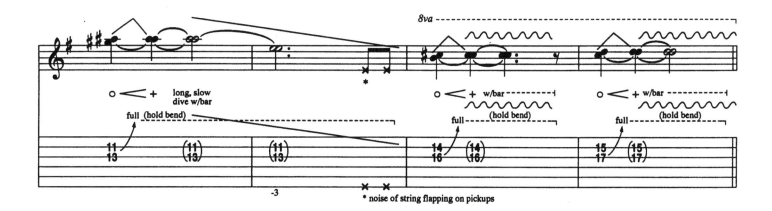

* noise of string flapping on pickups

Let's Get Phrasey!

As the 24 examples you've seen so far have clearly revealed, because you have total control of the Wah's rate of sweep and relative position, you can use this pedal to alter the tone, perceived rhythm, phrasing, and emphasis of your playing in quite a significant way. This can, of course, be done haphazardly or musically. It goes without saying that the latter approach is the way to go! If thought and taste prevail, the Wah-Wah can be used to highlight certain notes and add dazzling tonal contours to your playing in a highly desirable and also musical way.

One method of tonally sculpting a passage with your Wah is by using it to exaggerate the relative pitch of the notes. Confused? What I mean is this: Whenever you play an ascending part you close the pedal as you climb and vice-versa (*i.e.*, whenever you descend you begin to open it). Of course, the rate at which you open and close your Wah depends on two things: i) how dramatic or subtle you want the tonal effect to be, and ii) how long or short each ascent or descent is!

Figure 25 features the good ol' A minor pentatonic scale (A, C, D, E, G) and has you slowly rocking your pedal forwards (*i.e.*, from full bass to full treble) as you ascend and backwards as you descend.

Figure 25

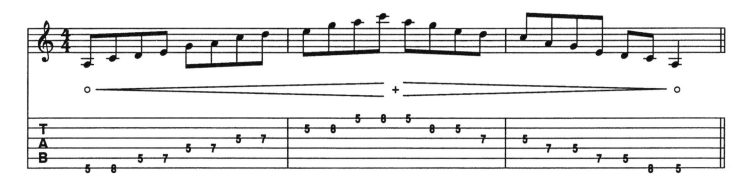

Figure 26 is a short but meandering E minor blues run that will tax your tone-sculpting abilities a hair, and Figure 27—an ascending/descending arpeggio passage that outlines a C, D, Em progression—will probably drive you to drink due to its syncopated nature.

Figure 26

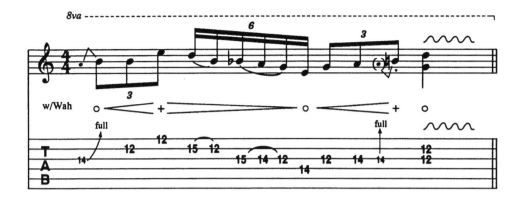

Figure 27

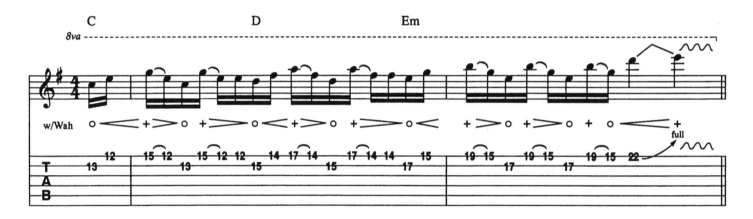

Rhythm 'n' the Blues!

Since the discussion has moved away from solely tapping your foot in time, I'm sure that a couple of the Wah-Wah ideas I've thrown your way have caused you extreme frustration—I mean, Figure 27 alone is a problem child of the highest order. If you're having difficulty articulating some of these examples, don't worry. Let me explain...

Moving your foot in a way that's rhythmically different from the straightforward "1 and 2 and 3 and 4 and" pulse of the music while doing something completely different with your hands ain't easy. But developing the required skill to be able to do things with your fingers and feet that are completely rhythmically independent is possible. Hell, if a drummer can develop this sort of hand/foot coordination then so can we!

So, please don't get discouraged if a Wah maneuver like the devilishly tricky one revealed below in Figure 28 doesn't come to you instantly. Instead, grit your teeth in true John Wayne fashion and apply the "three sacred Ps"—Practice, Patience, and Perseverance. If you do this you'll be fine, I promise! Once you've developed the ability to rock your foot in any rhythm you like, regardless of the song's backbeat and what your hands are doing, the only limit on your Wah-Wah work will be your musical creativity and imagination.

Figure 28

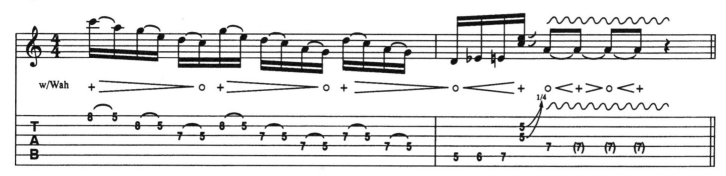

Mix 'n' Match

Once you're fairly confident with all the Wah tricks you've learned so far, the next step is to start mixing 'n' matching 'em in a way that will enhance your music. Of course, it goes without saying that there are no rules of thumb here. Each and every Wah-Wah moment that crops up will be different, so it's up to you to decide what will work best.

Figure 29 shows how Jimi Hendrix effortlessly switches from a quarter-note foot-tapping Wah pattern to a repeated slow opening of the pedal during his outro lead in "Up From The Skies."

Figure 29

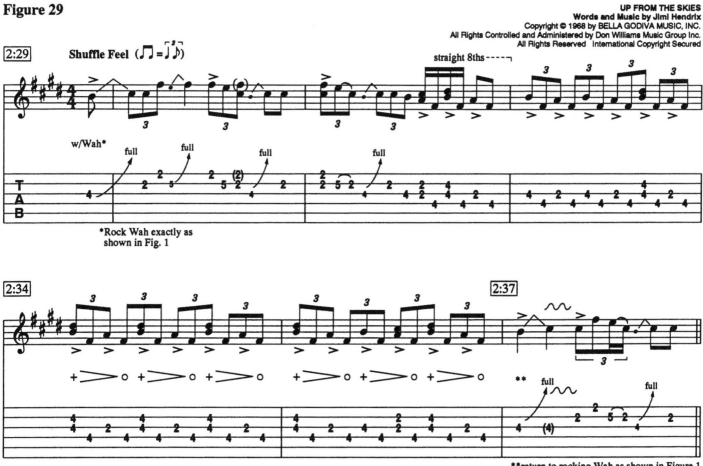

As promised at the start of this section, we're gonna close this chapter by jamming on what is arguably the finest piece of Wah-Wah work ever recorded—the first 12 bars of Hendrix's "Voodoo Child (Slight Return)." This passage has been transcribed in Figure 30, and as you can see, I've included Wah-Wah directions. At first glance it may appear that Jimi's use of the pedal is almost haphazard; but when you listen carefully to this monumental moment, you immediately realize that this great man knew exactly what he was doing. Hendrix's Wah inflections complement his playing to perfection. And that, in a nutshell, is what it's all about!

Figure 30

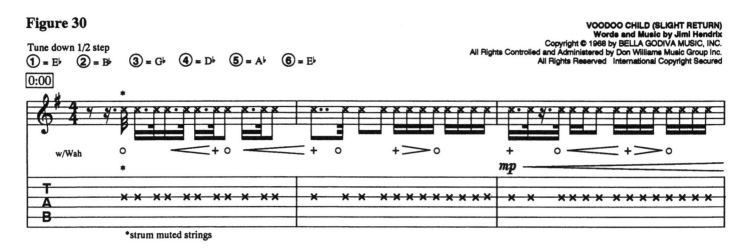

*strum muted strings

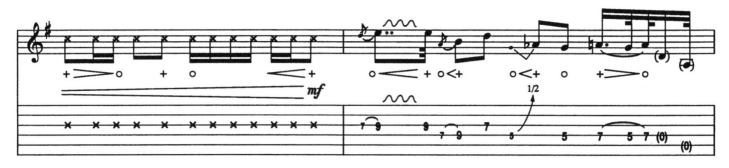

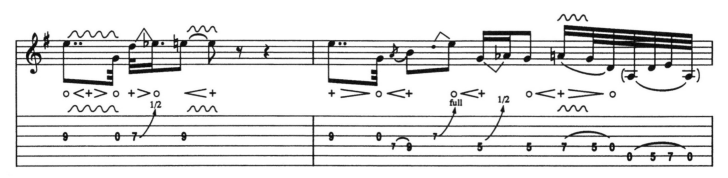

CHAPTER 3

Nine Killer Wah-Wah Solos from Past to Present!

Pre-Playing Pep Talk

In the pages that follow you're gonna get hit with note-for-note transcriptions of nine of the greatest Wah-Wah solos ever recorded—from the ground-breaking work of Messrs. Hendrix and Clapton in the late sixties right the way up to the present-day pedalings of Kirk Hammett, Slash, and Edward Van Halen! To enable you to practice some of these lead breaks with a guitar playing friend (or a tape recorder!) playing the backing, I've provided you with transcriptions of the rhythm guitar parts for six of the nine solos: "White Room," "Alive," "Mr.Brownstone," "Man In The Box," "Miracle Man," and "Enter Sandman." Also, to aid you further in this worthy learning task, CD counter readings have been included every four bars as landmarks that will help guide you through each solo.

Just so you know, when choosing these nine Wah-Wah leads (not an easy task, believe me; there are so many marvelous examples to pick from!) I purposely leaned towards ones that contained cool licks and runs that could be "stolen" and used in your own playing if you so wish. So, if you hear something you like, don't be bashful; plunder away with no remorse! Let's face it, we all "borrow" ideas from time to time—even the greats do it! That's how we learn!

In the first solo of this section, Jimi Hendrix's landmark lead break in "Voodoo Child (Slight Return)" (*Electric Ladyland*), I've included some Wah-Wah usage guidelines in the transcription. For the remaining eight, however, I haven't done so—you're on your own! Why am I doing this cruel and heartless thing? Because I want you to develop your ear for the Wah-Wah, that's why! So, listen and learn. Having said this, I will be kind enough to let you know when the pedal is switched on and off, 'cos in the couple of these solos the Wah-Wah isn't used throughout.

Helpful Hints!

The good ol' adage "if you can't hum it then you sure as hell can't play it" is one I firmly believe in, 'cos it's 110% true! So, don't rush into these leads like a bull in a china shop, otherwise you'll end up achieving little. Instead, try putting your guitar down and listening to the lead break you're working on over and over until it's planted firmly in your gray matter. It would also be wise to master the solo without using your Wah-Wah at first. And if achieving this means learning the thing one or two bars at a time, don't be afraid to do so. Once you've got the notes and phrasing down, it's time for you to add in the Wah-Wah magic.

Oh yeah, before you start wailing away, there's one other thing you should be aware of: Although the excerpts and solos that follow have been transcribed by some of the best guys out there (Wolf Marshall, Jesse Gress, Andy Aledort, Joff Jones, Dave Whitehill, Jimmy Brown, John Tapella, Dave Celentano, Andy Robyns, Jim Quinn), the art of transcription is, has been, and always will be highly subjective. So, if you hear some of this stuff slightly differently from how it's been written out, don't be afraid to go with your gut instinct. Good luck!

Solo 1: "Voodoo Child (Slight Return)"

Words and Music by Jimi Hendrix

To a great many guitarists, Jimi Hendrix's 1968 album *Electric Ladyland* was his crowning glory. Backed brilliantly by the other two members of The Jimi Hendrix Experience, Mitch Mitchell on drums and Noel Redding on bass, and aided by engineering legend Eddie Kramer, Jimi "produced and directed" this musical masterpiece.

(Courtesy of Warner Bros. Records Inc.)

Of all the remarkable recordings on *Electric Ladyland,* one that really stands out is "Voodoo Child (Slight Return)." What follows is a transcription of the twelve-bar solo that appears in the middle of the song. The key here is E minor, and for the bulk of his lead break Jimi sticks with the trusty E minor pentatonic scale (E, G, A, B, D). In bars 5 and 6, however, he uses the E Dorian mode (E, F#, G, A, B, C#, D). If you manage to nail this one you'll truly "kiss the sky!"

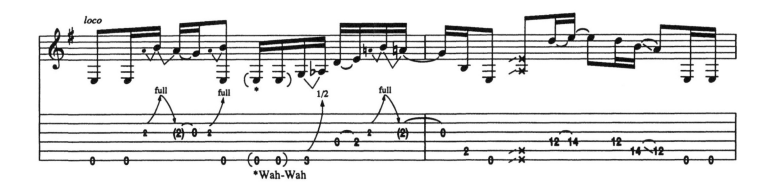

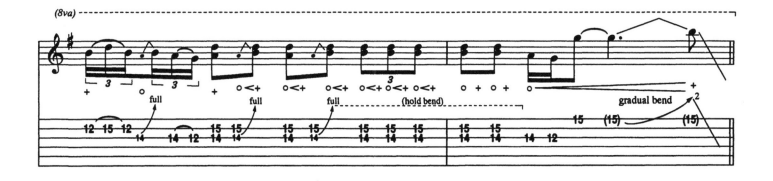

Solo 2: "White Room"
Words and Music by Jack Bruce and Pete Brown

"E.C. is God" was a piece of graffiti often seen in England during the late sixties and early seventies and when you listen to Eric's playing with The Yardbirds, John Mayall's Bluesbreakers, and Cream during that era, it's easy to see (or should I say hear!) why. The emotion Clapton conveys to the listener through his soloing is quite simply staggering. Along with Hendrix, Page, and Beck, the role Eric played in the evolution of rock guitar playing as we know and love it today is immeasurable. For instance, Edward Van Halen has always cited Clapton as a major influence and, apparently, can still fire off Eric's unforgettable "Crossroads" (*Wheels Of Fire*) solo note for note in a heartbeat!

As stated earlier, E.C.'s Wah-Wah work on Cream's "White Room" and "Tales Of Brave Ulysses" is considered a major landmark in the history of the effect. As we've already seen in Chapter 2, his tremolo-like use of the pedal during the pre-chorus of "White Room" is a stroke of genius. What follows is a transcription of the scintillating Wah-Wah solo he closes the track with. The key here is D minor, and Eric leans mostly on the D minor pentatonic scale (D, F, G, A, C); but he does throw in the flatted fifth (A♭) of the blues scale and the major sixth (B natural) of the Dorian mode from time to time. Providing you use your ears, you should be emulating this excellent lead in no time. Enjoy!

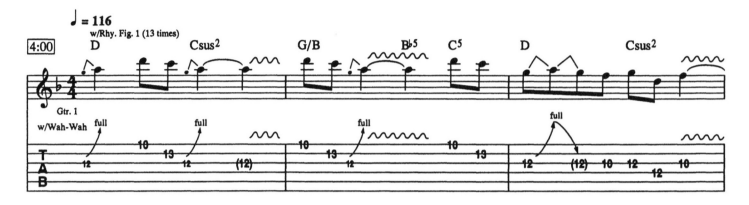

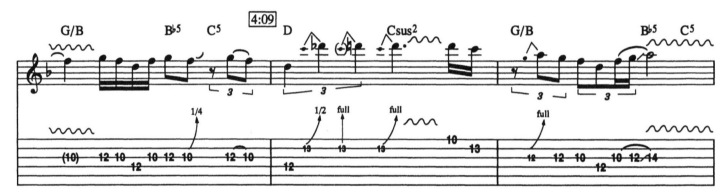

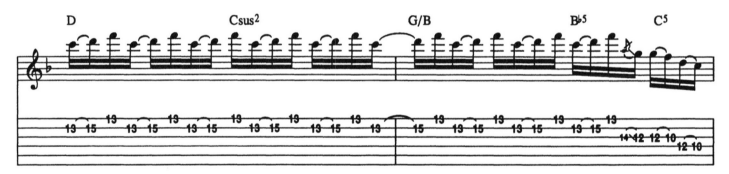

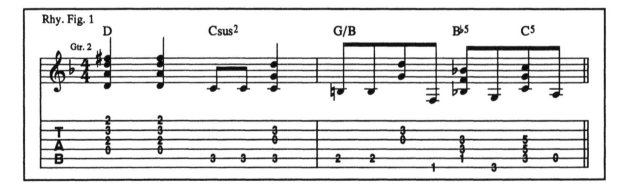

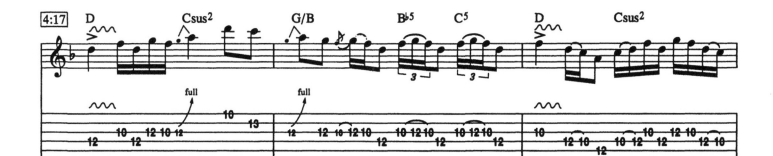

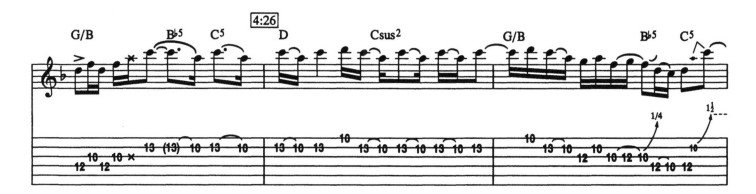

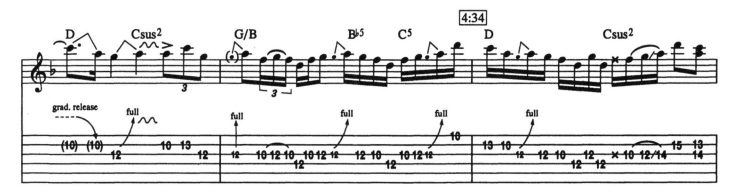

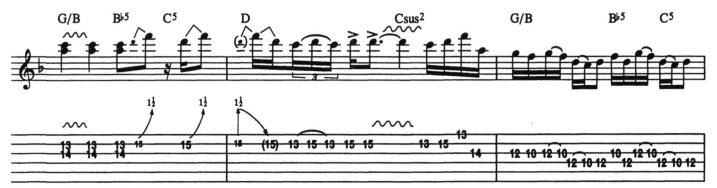

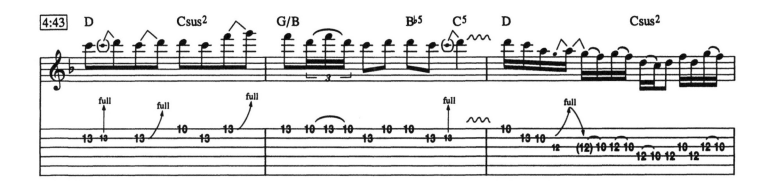

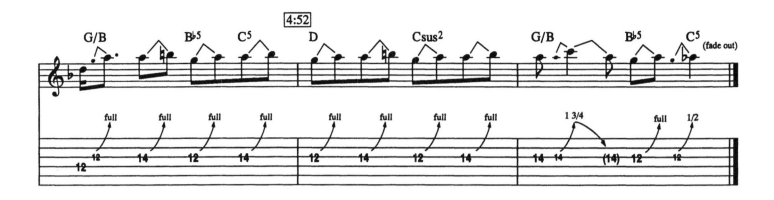

Solo 3: "Say What" (live)
By Stevie Ray Vaughan

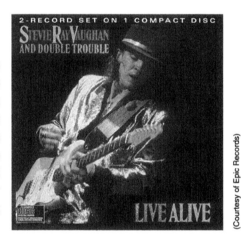

(Courtesy of Epic Records)

Stevie Ray Vaughan was, without question, one of the finest exponents of the blues to ever grace this earth. His ability to speak volumes with a few choice notes was almost uncanny as his all-too-brief recording career proves time after time. As good as his studio works are, though, like all great musicians, Stevie really came into his own when performing live. As if charged up by the electric excitement generated by the band, the music and the audience, Stevie's inestimable playing skills would hit new heights as he pushed both himself and Lenny, his beaten-up but beloved '64 Strat, to the very edge.

Just like one of his biggest icons, Jimi Hendrix, Stevie Ray Vaughan was an expert at using the Wah-Wah. In fact, he owned one of Hendrix's pedals and used it, along with another unit, on one of his most memorable Wah-Wah excursions ever: the instrumental "Say What" (*Soul To Soul*), which is a tribute to Jimi's "Rainy Day, Dream Away" (and the reprise "Still Raining, Still Dreaming") (*Electric Ladyland*). The following is the opening twenty-five bars of the explosive version of "Say What" that appeared on Stevie's 1986 live album *Live Alive*. By the way, it may interest you to know that both versions of this song were nominated for the "Best Rock Instrumental Performance" Grammy.

"Say What" is basically a twelve-bar blues in the key of C. In keeping with his blues-based roots, Stevie's guitar lines have been constructed using the following two scales as building blocks: C minor pentatonic (C, E♭, F, G, B♭) and C major pentatonic (C, D, E, G, A). Notice how he uses exaggerated finger slides to end certain notes (*e.g.*, the C note at the 10th fret of the D string in bar 4), adding a vocal-like edge. If you're interested in learning the rest of this great rendition of "Say What," a full transcription can be found in the Hal Leonard book *Stevie Ray Vaughan "Lightnin' Blues 1983–1987."*

Tune down 1/2 step

① = E♭ ④ = D♭
② = B♭ ⑤ = A♭
③ = G♭ ⑥ = E♭

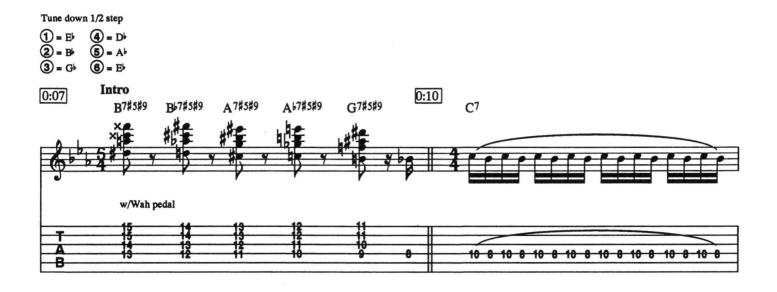

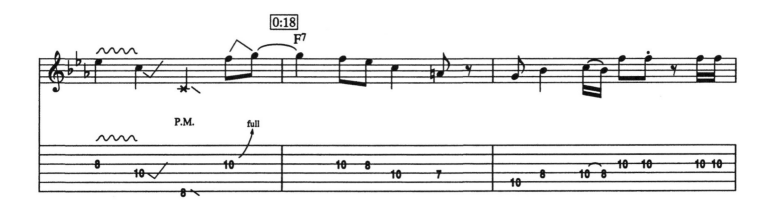

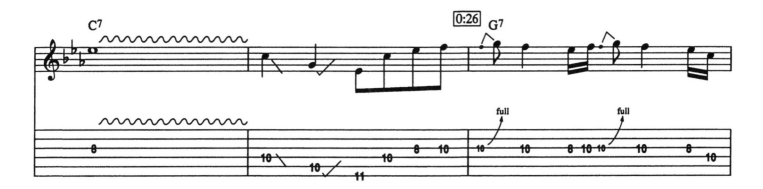

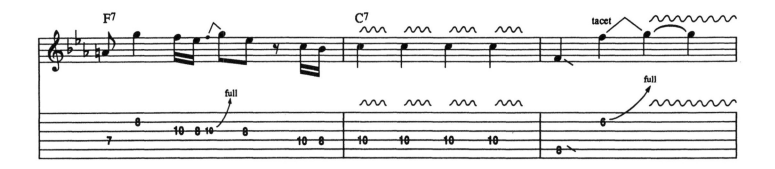

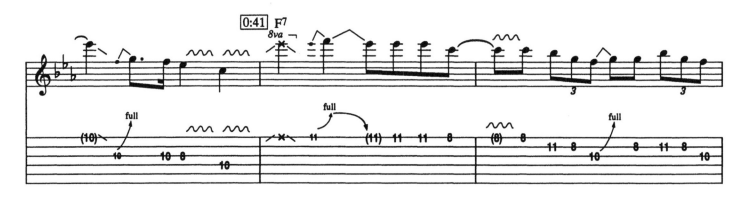

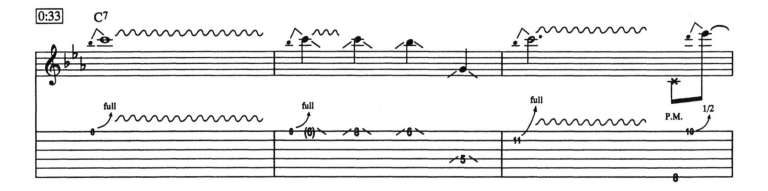

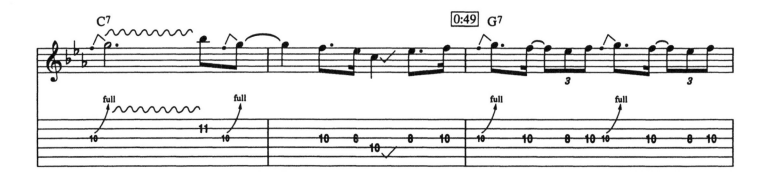

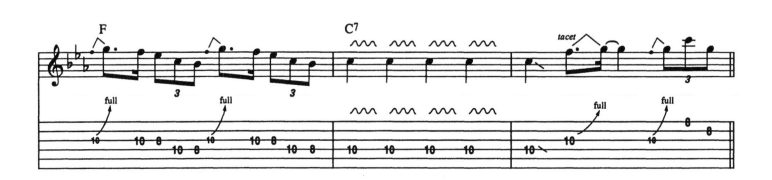

Solo 4: "Mr. Brownstone"

Words and Music by W. Axl Rose, Slash, Izzy Stradlin', Duff McKagen and Steven Adler

Alongside Pearl Jam, Def Leppard, AC/DC, and Metallica, Gun N' Roses are about as big as they get in the rock world. They've sold tens of millions of records and sell out arenas in all corners of the globe within hours! One of the many appealing aspects of the band's music is the no-nonsense, melodic, blues-based lead work of their guitarist Slash—the man responsible for making the Les Paul guitar a major force in the six-string kingdom again.

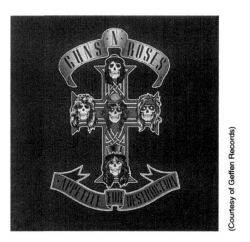

Like his searing solos, Slash's setup is uncluttered by anything unnecessary. All he basically does is plug his Les Paul into his Marshall stacks with nothing in between 'em except a Crybaby or two—believe it or not, he has no fewer than seven Wahs scattered about the stage so he is free to roam wherever he wishes!

The solo in "Mr. Brownstone" a great example of Slash's Wah-Wah work in action. The first eight bars are in F# minor, and then for the next three bars he follows the key changes implied by the rhythm guitar part—G minor (bar 9), C minor (bar 10), and D minor (bar 11). In bar 12 of the solo, Slash merely uses unison bends (a technique discussed in Chapter 3) to reinforce the root notes of the backing D5, C#5, B5, D5, G5 chord progression. Notice how he employs the Wah-Wah purely as a tonal filter in the last third of this lead. Also, check out the percussive "whacka-whacka" riff Guitar 2 plays in the final bar of this transcription.

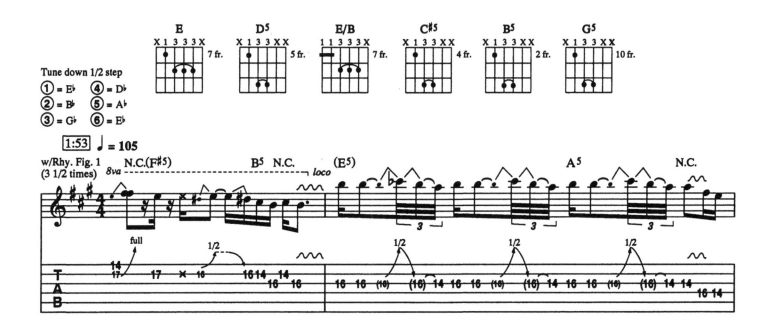

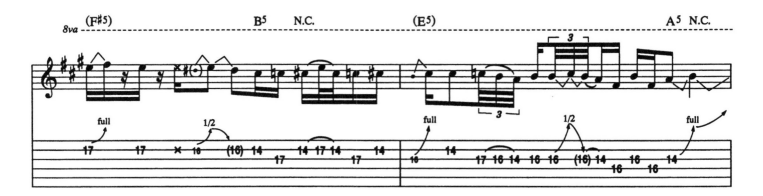

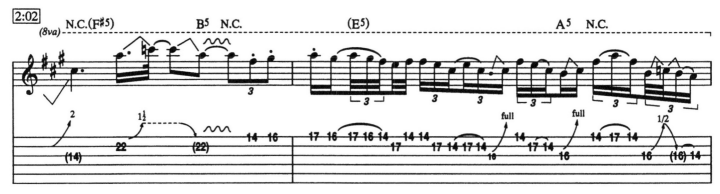

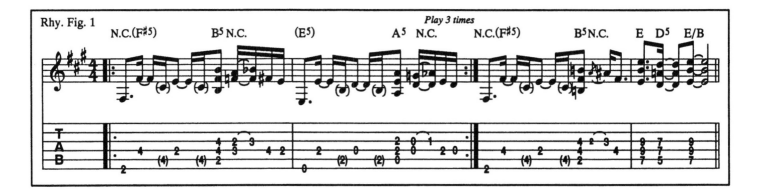

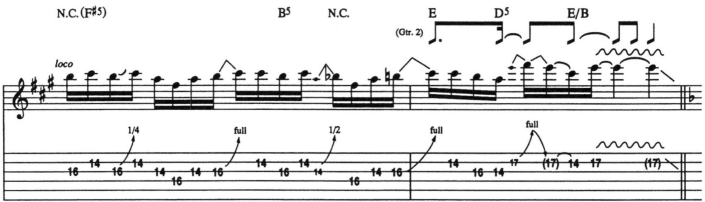

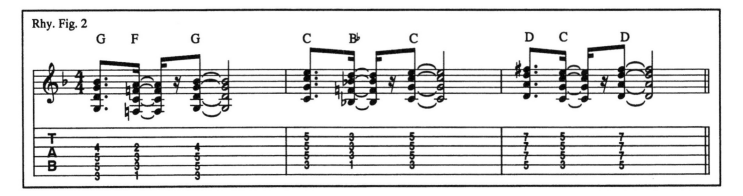

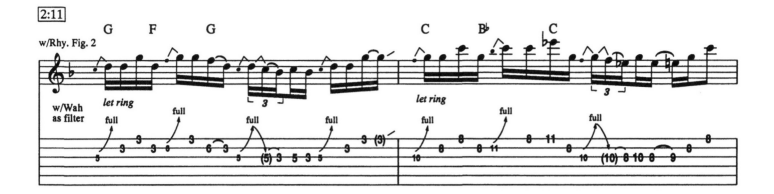

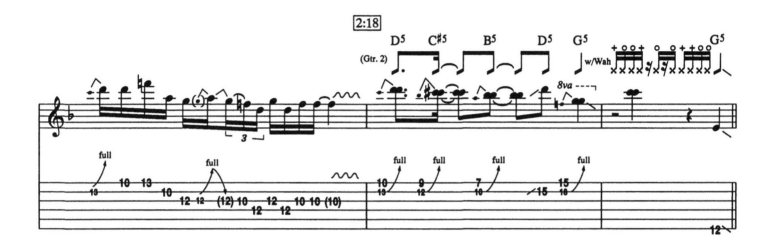

Solo 5: "Miracle Man"
Words and Music by Ozzy Osbourne, Robert Daisley and Zakk Wylde

Not only is the legendary Ozzy Osbourne one of metal's most colorful and beloved characters, he's also blessed with the ability of unearthing amazing unknown guitarists. Since leaving Black Sabbath in the late seventies, Ozzy has discovered three unbelievable six-string talents—Randy Rhoads (R.I.P.), Jake E. Lee, and Zakk Wylde. When Ozzy first discovered Zakk he was a mere twenty years old, but his fiery fretboard antics were anything but immature. Like Slash, Zakk's setup is straightforward—a Les Paul, a stack of Marshalls, and a few stomp boxes, including, of course, a Wah-Wah!

I've chosen Zakk's solo in "Miracle Man" (*No Rest For The Wicked*) for two reasons: First, it's excellent! And second, the Wah is used very sparingly indeed, an act which can often take a solo to the next level of intensity, as this one so clearly shows.

The first ten bars of the solo are in F# minor. During this time Zakk uses two scales: F# natural minor (F#, G#, A, B, C#, D, E) and the F# minor Blues (F#, A, B, C, C#, E). Then, at bar 11, the key changes to C# minor, and so Zakk calls on the same two scales but in the new key. Notice once again the use of unison bends to close the solo.

33

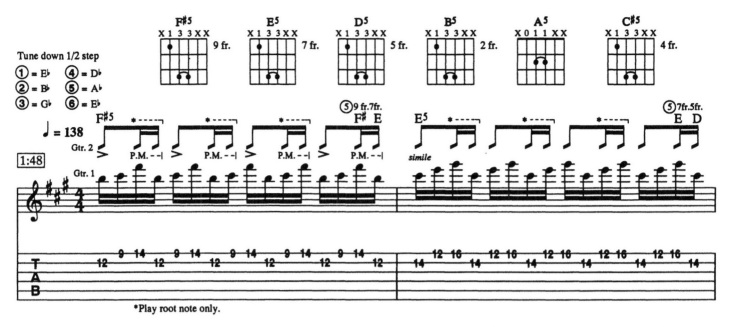

*Play root note only.

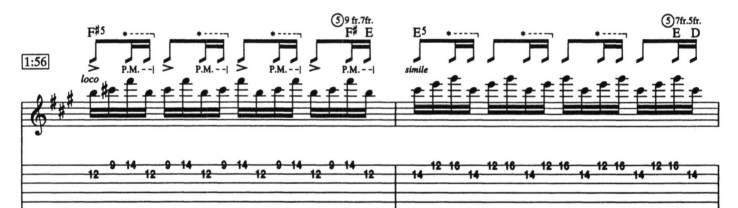

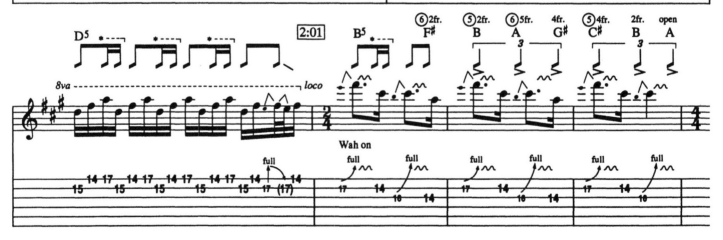

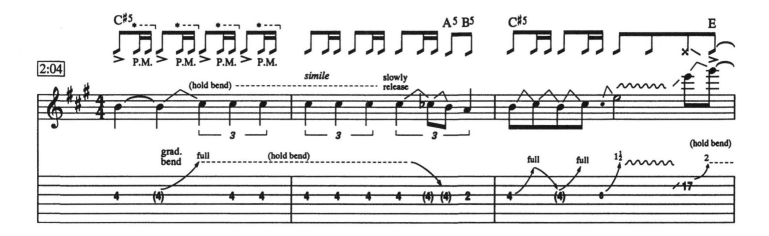

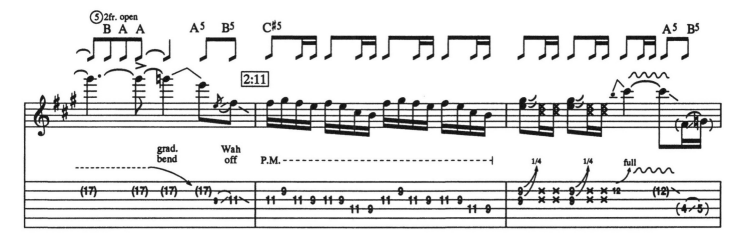

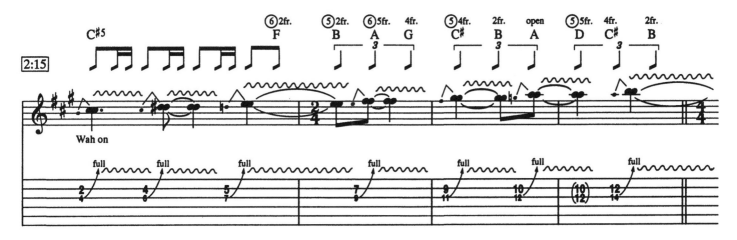

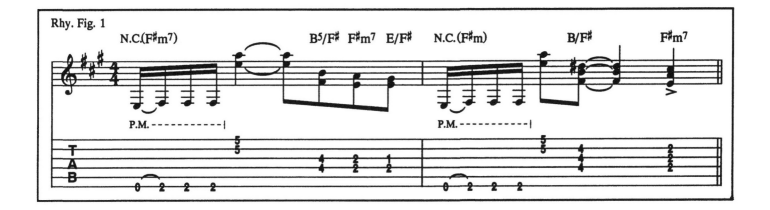

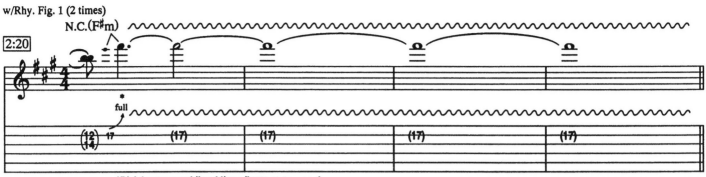

*Pick bent note while adding vibrato as on record.

Solo 6: "Man In The Box"
Lyrics by Layne Staley
Music by Jerry Cantrell

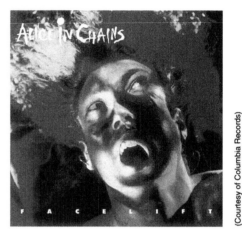

"I love Crybaby Wah—it's my main, number one effect. It makes the guitar talk." That's what Jerry Cantrell, lead guitarist and riff-master for Seattle grunge gods Alice In Chains, told *Guitar World* magazine. Not surprisingly, then, this great effect can often be heard in Jerry's playing. A perfect example of this is the first half of his "Man In The Box" solo.

The main scale used here is the E minor blues (E, G, A, B♭, B, D). As we discussed back in chapter two, the way Jerry slowly closes and then opens the Wah-Wah in bars 1 and 2 while trilling the same two notes (D and E) on the A string is a brilliant, ear-catching way to start this solo. He uses the idea of slowly opening the pedal again in bars 5 and 6 while repeatedly picking a bent string, and the effect is similarly devastating. At the start of bar 9 another guitar takes over the solo while Jerry sustains a string bend for nearly 4 bars—with a little help from some screaming feedback.

Tune down 1/2 step
① = E♭ ④ = D♭
② = B♭ ⑤ = A♭
③ = G♭ ⑥ = E♭

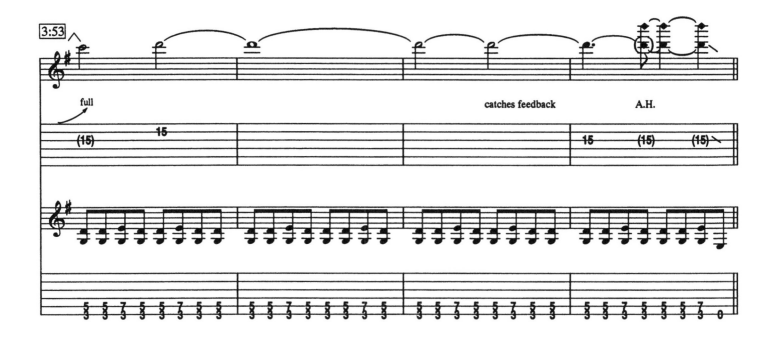

Solo 7: "Alive"

Music by Stone Gossard
Lyric by Eddie Vedder

(Courtesy of Sony Music Entertainment Inc.)

Aside from being one of the hard rock world's biggest selling debut LP's of all time, Pearl Jam's *Ten* is a glowing testament to the wonders of the Wah-Wah. In fact, thanks largely to the band's lead guitarist, Mike McCready, no fewer than seven of *Ten*'s eleven tracks feature the effect. The solo we're about to savor is Mike's lengthy salvo that closes the monumental hit "Alive." Here McCready proves in no uncertain terms that not only is the Wah-Wah alive (pun intended!) and kicking in the nineties, but so are lengthy solos that say something—like the leads in "Crossroads" (Eric Clapton and Cream), "Free Bird" (Lynyrd Skynyrd), "Highway Star" (Deep Purple), and Hendrix's "Machine Gun" (the song that directly influenced McCready's approach to the "Alive" lead), for example.

Mike waits until the end of the second bar of this thirty-seven-bar assault before he steps on his Wah-Wah but—surprise, surprise—once the sucker's been switched "on," it stays that way. The key here is E minor, and for the most part Mike employs the minor pentatonic scale (E, G, A, B, D) but does revert to the minor Blues scale (E, G, A, B♭, B, D) in bar 4 and the Dorian mode (E, F♯, G, A, B, C♯, D) in bars 21 and 33.

P.S.: In case you haven't noticed, this is the third lead break we've looked at so far that climaxes with unison bends. So if you don't use these suckers in your soloing, I suggest you start doing so pronto!

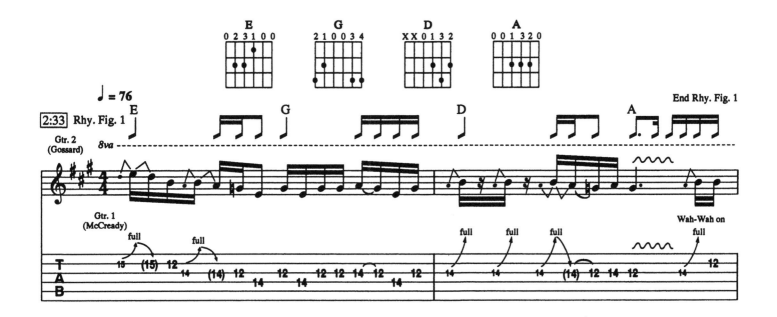

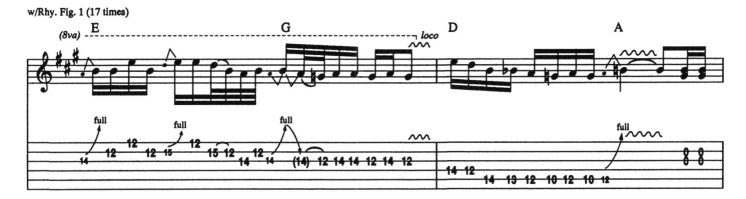

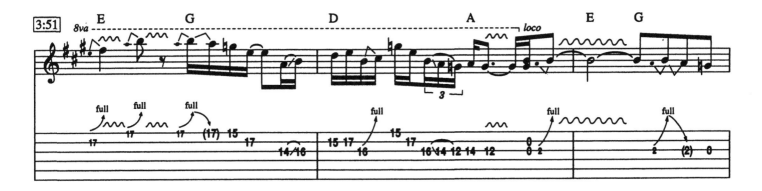

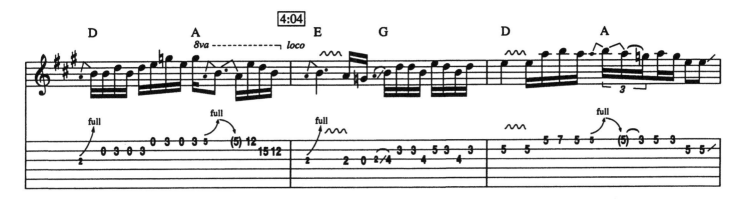

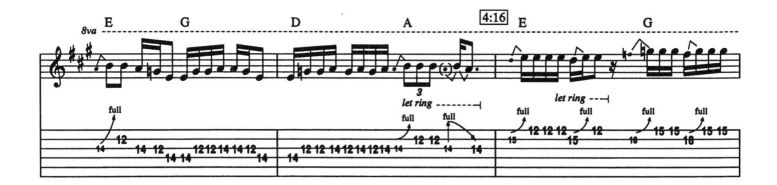

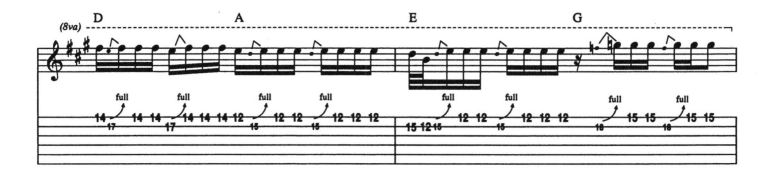

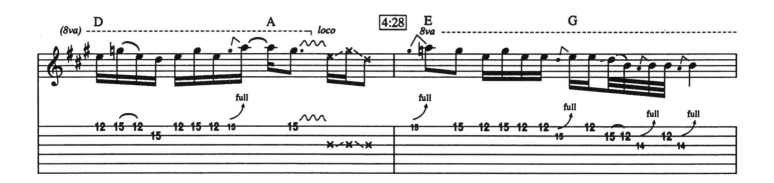

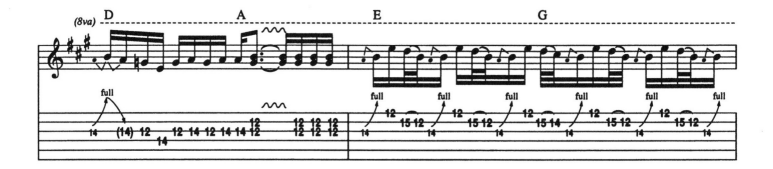

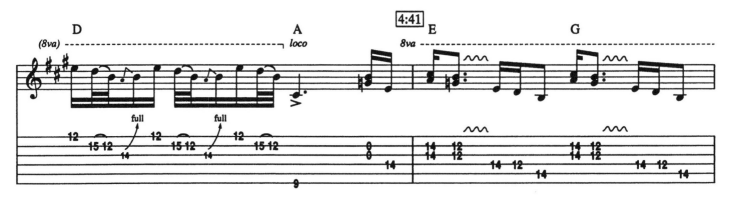

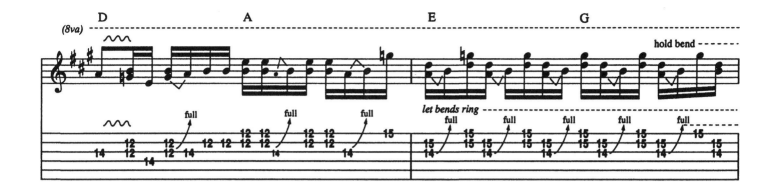

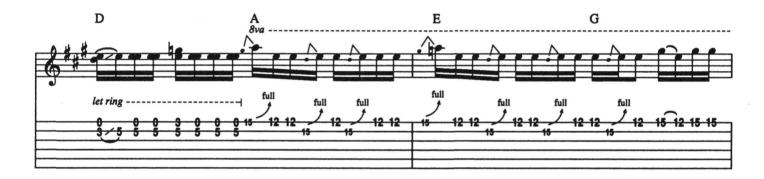

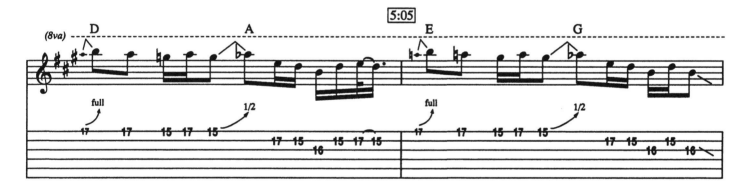

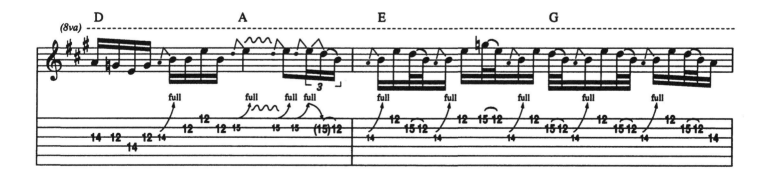

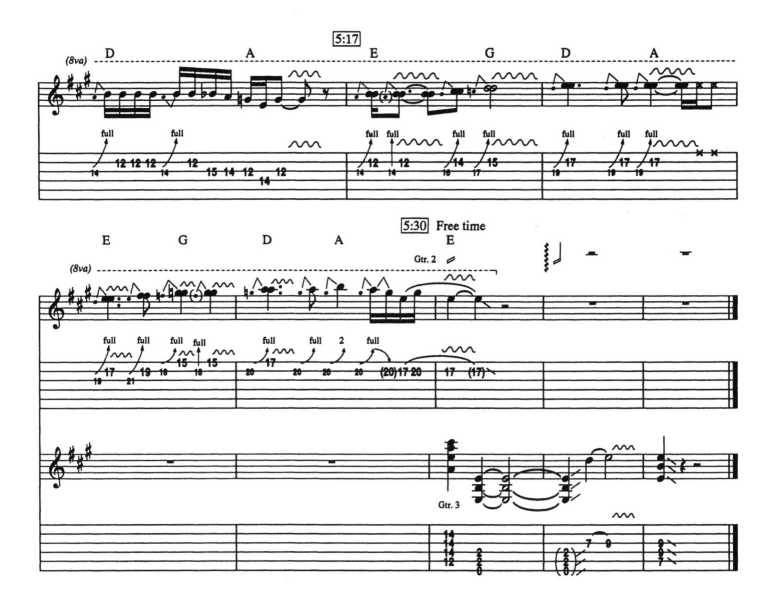

Solo 8: "Enter Sandman"

Words and Music by James Hetfield, Lars Ulrich and Kirk Hammett

In the darkened domain of heavy metal lead guitar, Kirk Hammett is the people's undisputed king. For the past six or seven years the author of this book's foreword has dominated "Best Metal Soloist" polls all over the world. In fact, at the time of writing this book, Kirk won the "Best Metal Guitarist" category in *Guitar Player* magazine's annual reader's poll for the fourth time. And, as usual, he did so by a landslide margin.

Ever since the release of Metallica's debut album, *Kill 'em All*, Kirk has been a champion of the Wah-Wah pedal. He's stepped on the device to creatively color a good many of his solos, and one of the most acclaimed examples of this is his bluesy blast in "Enter Sandman." For the first six bars of the solo Kirk uses the

E minor pentatonic scale (E, G, A, B, D), but changes to the Dorian mode (E, F♯, G, A, B, C♯, D) for the next two. Then, when Metallica's masterful rhythm guitarist, James Hetfield, modulates the sinister backing riff up a tone to F♯ minor (Rhythm Fig. 2) at the beginning of bar 9, Kirk ventures a tad "outside" by effectively playing in B minor—a seemingly strange move that works beautifully. Remember, amigo, sometimes there are no rules!

At bar 13 James stays in F♯ minor but changes his riff to Rhythm Figure 3. At this juncture Kirk reverts to a more logical scale—the F♯ natural minor scale (F♯, G♯, A, B, C♯, D, E). Then, when the key returns to E minor at bar 19, Kirk does likewise. Mastering this smoldering, emotion-filled solo will help improve your Wah-Wah technique greatly.

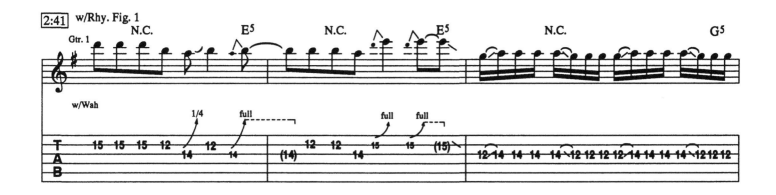

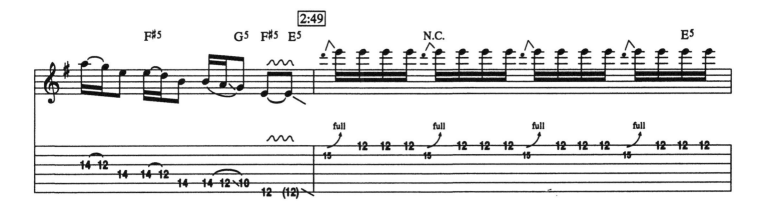

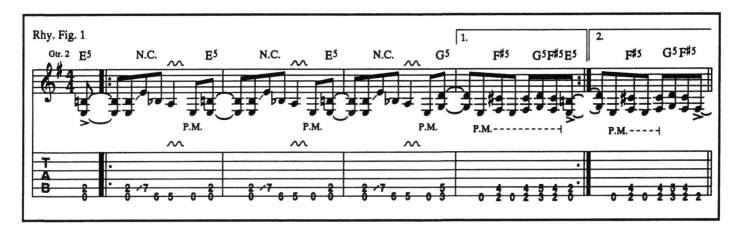

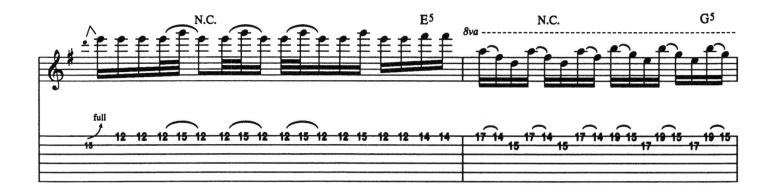

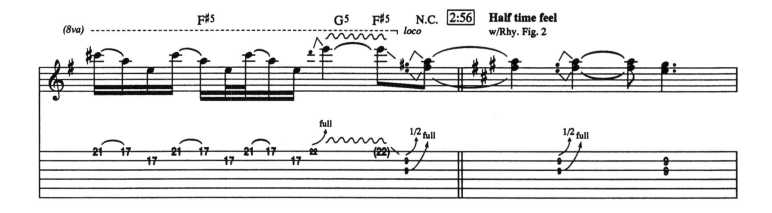

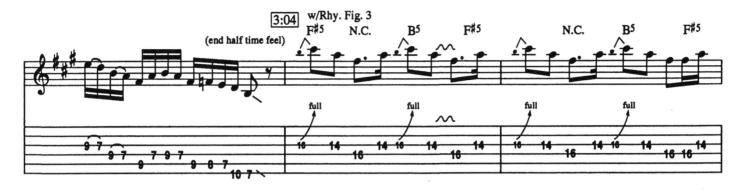

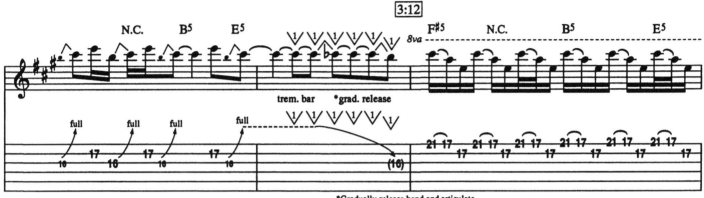

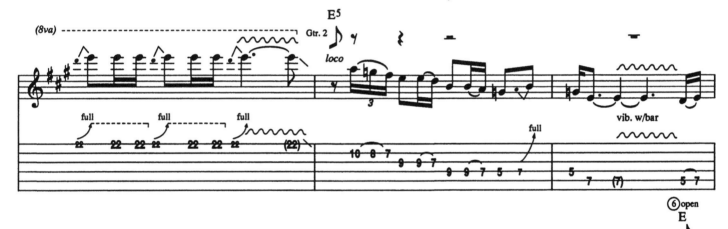

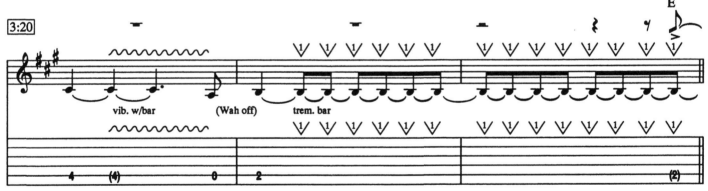

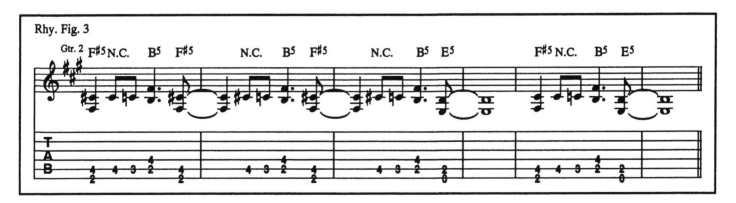

Solo 9: "In 'N' Out"

Words and Music by Edward Van Halen, Alex Van Halen, Michael Anthony and Sammy Hagar

Not since that quintessential quartet of Jimi Hendrix, Jeff Beck, Eric Clapton, and Jimmy Page stunned the six-string scene in the late sixties and early seventies has a single guitarist impacted the rock world as much as Edward Van Halen. As soon as *Van Halen I* hit the streets in 1978 everybody knew there was a new guitar god in town. His fiery and innovative use of harmonics, the whammy bar, and the two-handed tapping technique quite literally made him a legend overnight. Fifteen years and nine albums later (eight studio, one live), nothing has changed—Eddie is still king.

Now, Edward himself would probably be the first to admit that his name isn't one of the first ones to crop up when the conversation turns to the Wah-Wah. In fact, it might not be mentioned at all, because a lot of people consider him to be a "non user." While this notion is somewhat understandable, it's 111% wrong! For example, Edward can be heard employing one as a frequency filter/boost *à la* Michael Schenker in his "Cabo Wabo" (*OU812*) lead break, and the Wah-Wah stunts he uses to spice up his "In 'N' Out" (*For Unlawful Carnal Knowledge*) solo are quite simply stunning.

Out of all the lead breaks in this book, you'll probably find this twenty-bar burst of F♯ minor brilliance the toughest one to conquer—Eddie's whammy bar antics in bars 13 and 14 are particularly difficult, but don't let that put you off. Instead, take a deep breath and break the solo down into small, "bite-sized" segments. Then set about mastering each segment in turn. Adopting a "slow but sure" approach like this may take some time, but it *will* ensure that you emerge a winner...eventually!

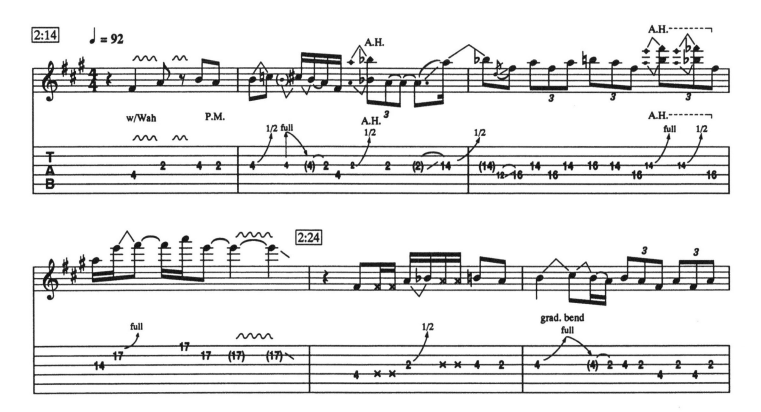

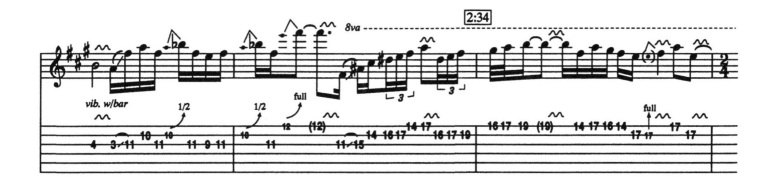

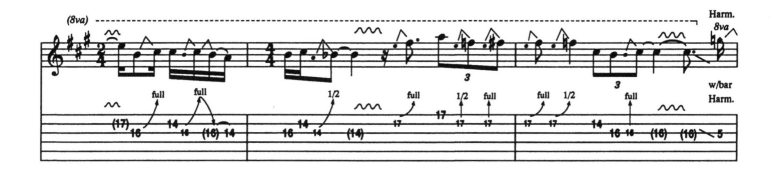

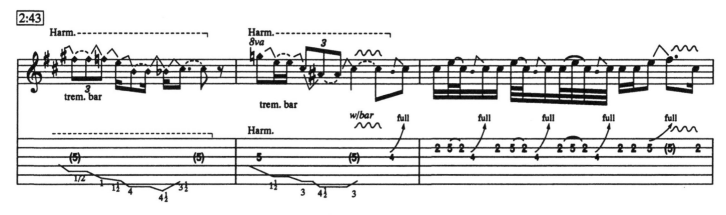

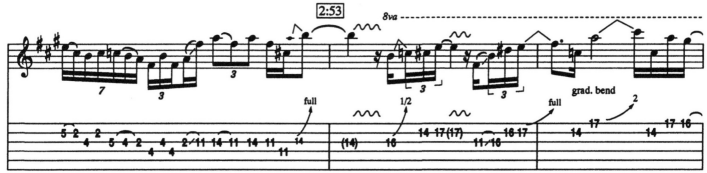

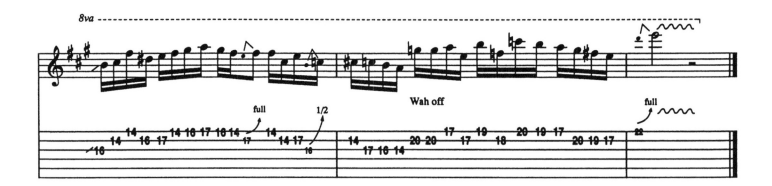

CONCLUSION

As stated at the very onset of our journey through Wah-Wah land, the aim of this book is a simple one: to open your mind to some of the many exciting possibilities the Wah-Wah pedal has to offer. As the excerpts and solos clearly show, this wonderful device can be used to paint a veritable rainbow of colorful musical moods, from subtle tonal enhancement to over-the-top, Wah-Wah-drenched outrage. As Jerry Cantrell so aptly put it: the thing can even make your guitar talk!

Hopefully, by now you're well on your way to getting a firm grasp of how greats like Hendrix and Hammett have used the Wah-Wah to their advantage and will have already started to incorporate some of the applications covered in your own playing. I'd also like to think that some of the marvelous licks and runs employed in the stuff we've looked at will have found their way into your ever-expanding library of "usable licks and runs."

Lastly, and most importantly, I sincerely hope that you had a lot of fun mastering the playing ideas presented in this book. If you did then I guess I did my job! See Ya!

The author would like to thank the following cool people for playing an important part in making this book what it is: Jim Dunlop Jr.; Brad Smith, Michael Wolfsohn, and John Cerullo at Hal Leonard; Smitty at Epic Records; J.; Dimebag; Tommy Victor; Joe Satriani; Dave Navarro; Walt, Andy, Amy, De De, Bobby, and Rob at Concrete Mgmt.; Erin Gravlin at Bill Graham Mgmt.; Jimmy Brown and Iwo Iwaszkiewicz at *Guitar World*; Nick, Tara, and Kaysie Bowcott; Pub Guinness; and, last but by no means least, the one and only Kirk Hammett.

This book is dedicated to the memory of Mike "Spike" Luty 'cos he would have dug it big time.

We miss you, bud.